Any Time

Any Place

Meditation

for your

Earthwalk

I0087824

By Susan Bradfield

First paperback edition ❧ December 5, 2008

ISBN: 978-0-615-25986-4 (paperback)

For all the teachers who shared their knowledge so generously, to all those who came as students and left as heart connected friends, and taught and passed forward as much and more than they received, our daughters who grew up and lived these principles, my circle of friends who have so patiently listened to my laments about bringing this to form, and my companion and honey who ultimately has been so very supportive of this endeavor.

Contents

Foreword

When you wish to climb a mountain, there are many trails from which you might choose. Meditation is similar to the mountain. It, too, has been around for a very long time in a variety of forms.

Lewis Bostwick developed the form of meditation I will be presenting here. Lewis is the founder of the Church of Divine Man and the Berkeley Psychic Institute.

In late 1978, my sweet friend and massage therapist, Parker, noted that I, at 26, was a mess, stressed both physically and emotionally. She suggested that I attend some classes she was taking with her sister in the East Bay. She assured me that I would find some peace of mind from the chaos and bombardment I was experiencing at work. I took these classes during the week and my husband, Bill, took them on Saturday mornings. This way one of us was always home with our girls.

I had previously been blessed to have Paula Gunn Allen, PhD., as a professor at the College of San Mateo. She had taken a liking to Bill and me. She would bring her children down from San Francisco to our little coastal hamlet on Friday afternoons. We would share a meal and usually end up at the beach with a small bonfire, hot chocolate for the children and hot tea for us. Sometimes we would go to the redwoods south of town. She mentored us for well over a year, sharing many different ways of looking at the world and life. I had no idea at the time what a foundation she was laying within us.

The following year, Professor Waldo Esteva joined the Ethnic Studies Department. His textbook was "The Teachings of a Yaqui Medicine Man", by Carlos Castenada. Building on all that Paula had gifted us with, I soared with this knowledge base.

I mention this part about Paula and Senor Esteva because Berkeley, located in the East Bay, has been known as a locale of adventure and alternative ways of viewing for many decades. Although I had grown up in the Bay Area, I lived on the peninsula side; I attended high school from 1966-70, participated in peace marches in Golden Gate Park, played in San Francisco at Winterland, the Fillmore Auditorium and Avalon Ballroom. I was basically a product of a sheltered San Francisco peninsula, middle-class albeit dysfunctional family. I was taking a step by attending these classes. A comfortable step, because I went with my friend, Parker, but still a life path altering step.

I was about to learn how to empower myself.

We enjoyed Meditation One, Two and Female Healing for me and Masculine Healing for Bill. Then it was time to decide about the clairvoyant training program. One also would take the Divinity classes to become an ordained minister. As we looked around the institute, we saw that some marriages did not survive the rigors of three class nights a week plus Sunday Divinity training and alternate Saturdays. We realized that in order for one of us to be home with the girls we would not be home together for the two year commitment. Bill offered to decline and just have me do the training. I, after further consideration, chose not to continue at this time and place.

It was not long, however, before I found myself in a weekend workshop at Senora's home. Senora and I had become instant friends when she arrived on the coast with her family several years prior. This workshop was led by two Shamanic practitioners, Peter and Harriet Calhoun, who offered an apprenticeship. After participating in several weekend workshops over the following six months, I discovered they were speaking a language that resonated deeply within me. I talked it over with Bill. With his blessing, I signed up.

This was a life changing experience for me. I left my family, for the first time ever, to go on periodic two or three week-long retreats. We studied in Canyonlands, Utah, where I did my four-day solo vision quest, in the Anza Borrego desert in California and the Grand Teton National Park in Wyoming. Backpacking in heights over 10,000 feet required six months of training for me after dwelling down at sea level. We built sweat lodges from scratch and sweated for hours. Some of our classes were held in these lodges. Rigorous hikes and classes in natural settings educated us to native ways of being with nature and all of her relations and kingdoms.

During my time in the apprenticeship, my father's health began to decline. We, my family, mother, sister and her family were to experience the effects of chemo and radiation on a loved one.

We also were to experience family dynamics. What was unfinished or ill at ease within my family, percolated to the surface. I had many opportunities to use the varied healing and spiritual tools I was gathering. My father taught me about death, choice and dying with dignity. Although I did not understand at the time, this was my first experience with supporting someone to cross over.

To backtrack just a bit, one night at the Berkeley Psychic Institute, during break time, Lewis happened to sit down next to me and ask how I liked my classes. He turned to me, looked me in the eye, and commented, "The only real quest in life is to take all of this life's information with you when you die. Then you will have ready conscious access to it in your next life. You gather your life force and exit through your crown when you die." I heard his words but had no idea what would come of them.

When my shamanic teachers informed me that I had an unusual teacher, I had no idea what they were referring to. They explained that one day I would understand about the realms of death and that I would facilitate people in their crossing over.

My father gifted me with the opportunity to do this service of preparing him to exit with all of his life force and exit through his crown as he left his body. Now, I began to understand what my shamanic teachers had referred to.

It was not so long after this that I found I was at completion with my apprenticeship, for now. I spent time reflecting on all that I had learned and gathered.

Eighteen months after my father's crossing, my mother's heart stopped one morning. Just that quickly she left my sister and me behind. My very foundation shattered.

Once again, the tools and experiences I had gathered slowly returned me to this world. Or so I thought. A rear-end collision from a drunk driver put me on notice that I had some serious healing to do on many levels. With my delightful little Mazda RX totaled out from under me, I stepped onto a path of gathering up my pieces.

During the year and a half of physical therapy, my physical health began to return, along with my mental, spiritual and emotional health. I read of a class to be given in Half Moon Bay through the Parks and Recreation Department. The description and wording caught my interest. A new teacher appeared in the form of Karen Wasco. Lo and behold, she had been one of Lewis's first students. We had an instant connection. We spent this year having weekly morning walks while I was recuperating.

Founding The Center of Healing and Intuition right in downtown Half Moon Bay, Karen afforded me the divine opportunity to redo the healing series and commit to the two-year clairvoyant training program. Karen resides in my heart to this day. She saw and knew parts of me I had yet to discover. With tremendous humor and knowledge she guided our class through this wonderful experience. As it came to pass, she and her teacher Lewis Bostwick passed from this earth a week apart.

I could go on and on, but my history is not the subject of this writing. I was encouraged to share a bit about myself. I sincerely hope this has served to do so.

So let us begin at the beginning.

I began teaching these classes in the early nineties. After guiding individual folks through the series on the coast, Bill and I moved from the coast. We traveled 10,000 miles around our nation and ultimately landed in Northern California between Mt. Shasta, Mt. Lassen and the Trinity Alps. It was there in a wooded oak and manzanita-covered land that I decided to offer the meditation classes through the local Junior College Continuing Education Program and through the Parks and Recreation Department.

You will find each subject or tool listed at the end of the class. This first series, Mediation One, is made up of seven classes. It has been a challenge to take the spoken and convert it to the written. I have been blessed by Michaele Benedict in her patient editing and by Matthew McEachen who has labored patiently on my behalf with the technical aspects of placing pictures and text. Fine tuning of the matter of the words has generously been provided by my loving circle of friends, cohorts and sisters of my heart: Chayo Wilson, who also supplied me with pictures and drawings used throughout this text, Barbara Rainforth, Darryl Brock, Izzi Wade, Mark Takata L.A.C., Connie Medhara, Marylin Watteyne L.C.S.W., who took the wonderful picture of the grounding tree, Dr. Sarah Slaughter, my daughters, Jamie and

Jennifer and their oh-so supportive husbands and my companion and honey of thirty-nine years.

Introduction

Meditation has been documented as a means to stress reduction. What do you think of when someone says they are going to meditate? Consider your initial response to this.

For some, a mat on the floor with the body positioned comfortably comes to mind. Others picture the body sitting comfortably in a Yoga position or chanting a mantra. There are many different ways to meditate. There are some common denominators. Breathing is one. The human body loves oxygen. Most folks breathe from their collarbone up when they are in stress mode. Sighing and yawning are a means of oxygenating our bodies. In Yoga, one of our teachers taught a four-part inhalation and then a four-part exhalation. I have found that our bodies just plain like it when we take nice slow deep breaths into our abdomen. I am certain there are many medical explanations for this. This could be the subject of a whole book.

Comfortable body position is relative to each individual. I still find the lotus position to be a bit beyond my ligaments' stretch, but for some it would be right up their alley.

In the ideal world, we would all have minutes, perhaps up to thirty of them a day, to sit in quiet contemplation. The current reality of most folks' days is that they are lucky to have mere moments unto themselves.

The art of meditation is actually available to us **any time, any place,** if we become aware that it is connected to our breathing. We know that we all are breathing twenty- four hours a day. Unless we experience a difficulty with our breathing we leave it to our autonomic nervous system. This system also deals with stress when it impacts our body. Have you had an awareness of your belly tightening or a constriction in your throat or chest? These are the body calling to us. A deep breath down into your abdomen at that moment begins the reversal or calming within your body.

Meditation encourages each of us to remember that we as human beings are body and spirit. It is healthful for us to meet our world each day consciously aware of our body equaling human and our being reflecting spirit. There is an art in meditation of taking a deep breath and becoming aware of your being sitting in the center of your head. From this place you have access to your central nervous system. An image may be that of Houston control with your body being the shuttle. You are empowered with choice of how, where, why you focus your energy on to some person, place or thing.

Imagine your body remaining calm, in a relaxed state for the majority of your day. This is sooo possible.

Class One

Breathing, Imagining, Validating, Grounding, Centering, Running Your Energy and Your Upper Circuit.

There are basic principals that create the foundation of meditation. Breathing, grounding, owning the space in the center of your head, awareness of your chakras, aura and cords are some of the *tools* you will gather.

Breathing is primary.

We all breathe twenty-four hours a day, usually with very little consciousness directed toward this function. Actually, this appears necessary at this time. Imagine when we become busy multi-tasking if we had to remember to breathe! We would witness bodies fainting from lack of oxygen! Our autonomic nervous system keeps track of the requirement of the human body to breathe. What happens when we are busy doing life is that the human body experiences the stress of multi-tasking. We begin to breathe more shallowly. Our abdomen does not rise and fall with each breath. The body eventually screams at us, "Where is the oxygen?" We were only breathing to the depth of our collarbones!

One of the foundations of meditation is the art of a taking in a slow deep breath followed by a slow exhalation. In this moment, just draw in a nice, slow, deep breath and slowly exhale. Ahh, the body does appreciate having some oxygen flow to its cells.

This particular meditation technique was designed to be done **at any time, in any place, with one's breath.** I believe now that Lewis had insight into what was coming in terms of the pace of daily living. The 70's were so very mellow compared to the pace we engage at now.

~~~~~~~~~~*Technique*~~~~~~~~~~

Gently take a look around the room or space you are in. Your body likes to know where it is before it is comfortable and willing to just close the eyes. Now you are going to close your eyes. When we close our eyes, we eliminate the sensory data coming in from our viewing of our world. Our other senses heighten, become more acute. We may become more aware of smells, temperature, and external sounds in our environment. Just allow these to register as you draw in a few more nice slow deep breaths.

"Imagine" is defined as: "to form a mental picture, conjecture, to think, to fancy." Imagine with your inner sight that a large suitcase has appeared in front of you. Into this suitcase gently drop in your mind's list of tasks, let your current worries and sense of exhaustion be released. With your ability to imagine, now allow the suitcase to melt into nothingness. Take a nice deep breath in.

Now create the sense of a container or tool box of some sort. Imagine a briefcase, sewing box, tackle box, picnic basket, jewelry box, satchel, whatever kind of container you would like. Once you have settled on your container, bring this image within an arm's distance of you and just let it be. You will fill it with your tools as you move through these classes.

Stop reading for a moment and take a nice deep breath. Notice what you are feeling. Distinguish what you are thinking from what you are feeling. Take another nice deep breath. Feel your body.

"*Validate*" is defined as: "to substantiate, to verify." Validate how your body is feeling at this moment. Would it like you to do something for it? Your body may desire more water for hydration, sleep for rejuvenation or exercise for your physical well-being??? Just by saying hello and asking your body, "What's up?" is a wonderfully nurturing act. Take in a nice deep breath and feel your feet on the floor.

We are Human Beings.

In other words we are **human = body** and **being = spirit**.

~~~~~~Grounding Cord Information~~~~~

Our great-grandparents and perhaps our grandparents knew all about grounding cords without ever calling them that. They were out and about on their land, feeding animals, tending gardens and crops. In many arenas they were connected to their earth.

Recently, since World War II, we as a nation have become more removed from the earth beneath our feet. It is our birthright to be connected to the land and the earth! We may now wish to bring consciousness to that connection. We are able to do this with the art of breathing, which we do all the time.

~~~~~~~~Getting Grounded~~~~~~~~~

"*Visualize*" is defined as: "to form a mental vision or image of."

Become aware of the base of your spine, near your sitz bones or as we sometimes hear it named, tailbone. Put your feet flat on the floor. With your eyes closed, gently draw a nice deep breath in and exhale out slowly. As you breathe, gift yourself with the opportunity to create your own unique grounding cord, here and now.

Gently imagine a connection from the base of your spine dropping down through the layers of earth toward its center. This cord may be made of whatever you wish.

For example you might have:

- a huge tree root,
- a light beam,
- an anchor on a chain dropping over the side of a ship holding it in place

Drawing by Justine Phipps, age 11

at the dock with a kerthunk as it hits the bottom.

14

You get it!

Each of us designs our own unique grounding cord.

Trust your body's inherent knowing. This cord connects us from the base of our spine to the center of the earth. When it connects to the earth's center there is a tactile or visual quality. It is our body's acknowledgement that it is grounded. It is like when the anchor hits the harbor floor, taking form from the base of your spine and dropping down into the earth. Or it may look like a giant redwood tap root, or a light beam, a chain, or a cord, whatever You would like to imagine dropping down through the layers of the earth to its core to connect. Your grounding cord is like a lightning rod through which the earth neutralizes your released energy. When your cord reaches the center of the earth there is a connection. So it is with whatever form your grounding cord takes as it connects to the center of the earth. We feel so much more at ease and in charge of our lives when we are grounded.

Trust your Body.

Feel where your body is tense and let go. Drop your tension down your grounding cord. This is like a garbage chute in a multi-

Photo by Marylin Watteyne

15

storied building. With your grounding cord switched on, let your worries and angst drop down your cord. Notice, what does your grounding cord look like? How does it feel to your body? Use the body on page 19 to draw your unique grounding cord.

Take a nice deep breath and just validate and congratulate yourself for making your own unique grounding cord.

~~~~~~Center of your head: Ownership~~~~~~

With a nice deep breath, you will now create your own unique sanctuary. This is the room in the center of your head. Consider having your own "command central" with a 360 degree view. With your eyes closed, breathing in and out slowly and deeply, imagine your room. Take your time to locate and observe it. How would you like it to be? What does it look like? How does it feel? Is anyone else in there with you? If so, say hello to them and then ask them to go outside. Everyone has the center of their own head to hang out in. This is YOUR space and you have now claimed it. Make this space comfortable for yourself. Imagine a chair or couch to command from.

Here your mind may take a rest, stop the thinking and incessant chatter, to just BE. Our mind may process 22 thoughts per second. How healthful to give it a rest time. You may replenish yourself in this space.

One spirit to one body or your spirit in your body.

With a nice deep breath, plunk yourself down into your oh so comfortable chair that you have placed in the center of your

16

room. Become aware of the part of you that is able to gaze about this room.

This is your Being.

This is the other half of **human being**. Say "Hello" to your being. Sitting in your custom designed chair, allow two big picture windows to form in front of you. As your being observes, looking out of your big picture windows, what do you see? Breathe in and out.

This is *Present Time*.

When your being is present in the center of your head, looking out of your big picture windows, you are in the present moment.

~~~~~~~~~~~*Running your Energy* ~~~~~~~~~~~~

With a nice deep breath, gently draw in a warm golden current of energy from above your head. Inhale this golden energy through the top of your head where your soft spot was when you were a baby. Allow it to fill in your nooks and crannies, as you **inhale** this golden energy, in, down along the back of your spinal column, like melted butter on a toasted English muffin. As you **exhale** this golden energy it loops up the front of your spinal column, comes to your throat and pauses, then it washes out across your shoulders, down your arms to your hands.

Feel your hands. Allow them to face each other without touching. What do you feel? Continue to take slow deep breaths, in and out. This energy that you feel is YOUR life force energy. Slowly move your hands toward each other and then slowly apart. Remain aware of your hands and what you are experiencing between them. We all have this life force energy moving through us. Does your life force energy have a quality to it? Is there density? Are you aware of any color? Identify how this feels to you.

Now we are playing with our own CHI. Karen referred to this as our CHI* ball. This ball that we may feel between our hands when we run our upper circuit is made up of our life force energy.

This is your upper circuit.

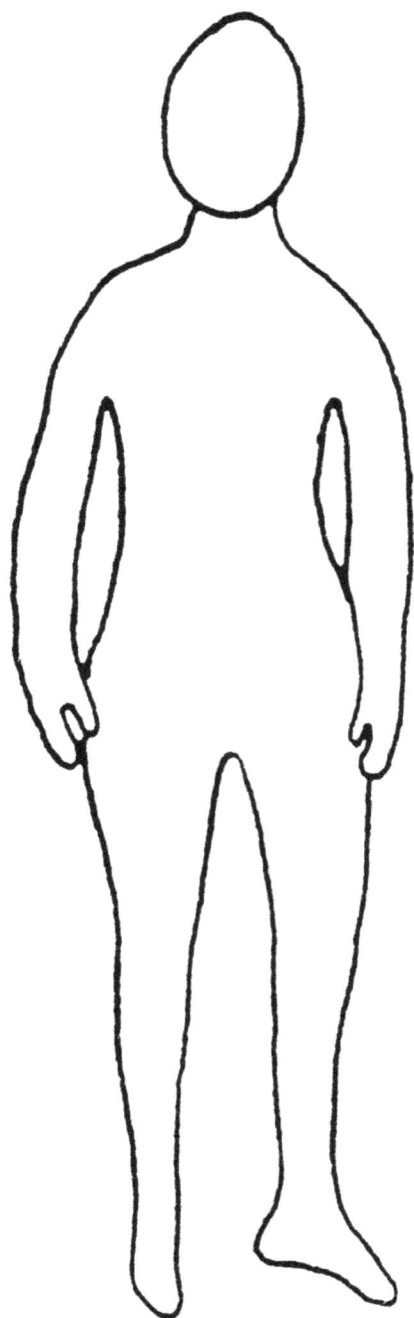

With a nice deep breath remember your toolbox. Gently place awareness of each of your newly acquired tools into your container. Allow your toolbox or container to gently rest in your room in the center of your head.

You now have these *tools*, defined as "a device, machine, means or instrument" available to you **any time, any place** to assist you in being more in charge of your experiences:

1. your unique grounding cord
2. the center of your head
3. the presence of your being in Present Time
4. your upper circuit.

* It is a testament to Karen's wonderful humor. She named her school, the Center for Healing and Intuition, so the nickname would be CHI.

Class Two

Information, Your feet, Lower Circuit, Calling Back Your Energy, Attention and Focus, Exercise of Feeling your Upper and Lower Circuits, Grounding
~Prove It Exercise~

If you have two pieces of chocolate, or a kind of candy you like, available, it is handy to pop one in your mouth at the beginning of this class. If you would rather, you may use a fragrant flower. Smell its scent.

With a nice deep breath, say hello to your grounding cord. Gently be aware of your grounding cord from the base of your spine dropping down into the earth. Allow it to drop down through the layers as it moves toward the center of the earth. Plunk, it is connected. Take another nice deep breath and allow any friction, angst, frenetic emotion to just drop down your grounding cord. This is like dropping garbage into the garbage chute on the third floor of a building. It drops down into the big dipsy dumpster in the basement. This is how a human body releases static energy. It drops it down our own unique grounding cord. Allow your grounding cord to expand to the width of your hips.

At the earth's core this energy is transmuted. It is just energy, without the charge; it is neutral, once again. Your unique, individual tap root or grounding cord is connected. With your body grounded now, remember the suitcase, allow your lists and any pressing concerns to be released into the suitcase. This will allow you to be present for gathering this next set of information to you. Gift yourself with these moments of just being present as you read and breathe and do the exercises. You will find that your body will appreciate and be responsive.

"*Information*" is "knowledge derived from study or experience." "*Inform*" is "to impart information to; to imbue with a quality."

From the center of your head, remember your room and the sense of owning your world from your command central. Look around your room. If there is anyone else in here with you, say, 'Hello" and ask them to leave. They may go to the center of their own head. Claim your ownership of this very valuable space in the center of your head. "This is my space and I claim it". Luxuriate in this space. Let your mind have a rest. This is home for your spirit in your body. Human-being. One being in each body is how it works. With your Being sitting in its chair in the center of your room, look out of your big picture windows. This is your world in *Present Time*.

It is said in acupuncture that meridians have entry and exit points at the head, hands and feet. All of our organs, systems and parts are interrelated along these meridian lines that run through our body. At each cross point of the meridians an energy center is formed. In some arenas this is called a *chakra.* There will be more on *chakras* in Class Four.

Let us look at the foot reflex chart. In this exercise you will follow the arrows on each foot, 1 through 11. Gently, lovingly acknowledge your foot as you move your thumb in the direction of the arrows, along the pressure points on the meridians. We ask our feet to provide a foundation for us all of our days. We rarely stop and focus any thought on how they are doing.

Ten minutes on each foot is enough at one time. As you finish nurturing your first foot, make a fist and place it in

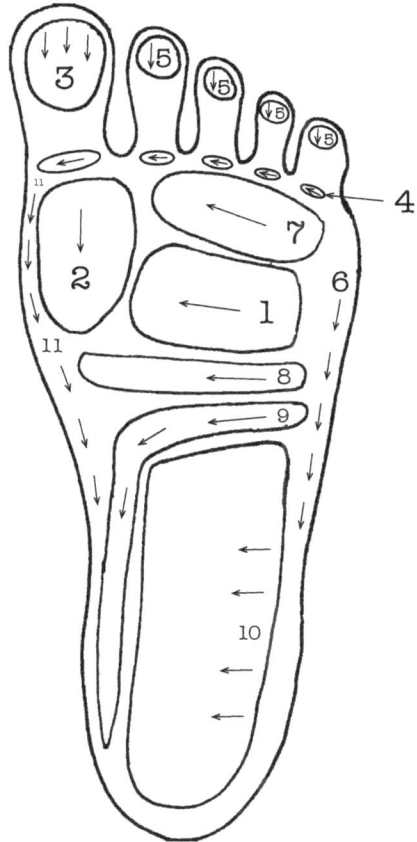

the arch of your foot. Say hello to this arch that supports your foot. This is an energy center where you will draw the earth's energies up through your feet into your body.

Do your second foot. Notice, is it tired or sore or the same as the first foot?

At the end of this foot's 10 minute nurturing, find your arch and say hello to it.

~~~~~~~~~Your Lower Energy Circuit~~~~~~~~~

Now with awareness of each of your two arches, gently draw in a nice deep breath. The energy will come up through your feet, up your calves and thighs, across your hips to your grounding cord. As you exhale gently, drop this earth energy down your grounding cord. You have created a loop, a connection to the earth. As you breathe in, you draw the earth's energy up through your feet and as you exhale, you drop it down your grounding cord. This creates your lower earth connected energy circuit. Note that if you have flat feet, you still have the place on your foot where your arch is.

~~~~~~~~~Running Your Energy~~~~~~~~~

Consider some person, place or thing that recently has been irritating to you. With a nice deep breath, draw the irritant to your grounding cord and as you exhale drop it down your cord. This works like Drano in a drain. The focus of drawing earth's energy in through your feet with your inhalation places the irritant at your grounding cord, and exhaling drops it down, in essence flushing it away, releasing it fully.

Now is a great time to

pop your second piece of candy into your mouth

or to take another slow luxurious sniff of your flower.

Take a piece of paper. Consider all that you have done since you woke up this morning. Begin to tear small pieces from your paper, representing all of the tasks you have done thus far this day. Place your pile in front of you. If you want, you may stand up and drop these around you. This is how we disperse our energy as we move through our day. We engage with people, places and things. We exchange energy. One phone call may take a sizeable chunk of our paper if it was filled with emotion. One ten minute drive around town where someone cuts you off or slams on their brakes in front of you, may take up a sizable chunk of your paper.

After reading this, close your eyes. Allow yourself to be totally present in the center of your head. Is your chair the most comfortable you can imagine? If not, make it so! It is free, so be as creative as you like. This chair is for your being to sit in.

One being in one body. You know, Human-Being or Body-Being.

Imagine a filter of any kind above your head. It may be a gold coffee filter, an oil filter, a finely woven colander, whatever kind of filter you might like. Your filter is put into place to separate any energy coming in that is not yours. It is a safety feature.

With this filter in place, about an arm's length above your head, CALL back your energy, attention and focus from all the places you have dispersed it. With a nice deep breath, allow your life force energy to come back to you, pass it through your filter and have it travel down the back of your spine and then up the front of your spine. It is following your upper circuit. Just as the oil in your vehicle lubricates its parts, this is your oil or life force energy which supports your body. Your own energy feels good: someone else's does not.

We interact with people, places and things all the time and disperse our energy or life force. We have the ability to call it back to us.

Back to the chocolate or flower.

How did the second piece taste as compared to the first?

How was the smell different now from your initial whiff?

When we are in present time with our Being in the center of our head, it is interesting to note how food tastes or scents smell. What most of us find is that when we are in *Present Time* our awareness of what we are eating, smelling, hearing, sensing is more acute.

~~~~~~~~~Running Your Energy~~~~~~~~~~

Once again after reading this, gently close your eyes and allow the memory of your upper circuit to come to you. This is your connection to your divine or higher self. With a nice deep breath, gently bring a warm golden channel of energy in through the top of your head, where your soft spot was when you were born. Inhale this delightful, nurturing energy down along the back of your spinal column. A little bit drops down your grounding cord, and as you exhale, bring it up the front of your spinal column to your throat, letting this golden energy flow out across your shoulders, down your arms to your hands.

Feel your hands! Then bring the golden energy back up to your throat, up over your face, washing your big picture windows, and on up and out of the top of your head at the front of your soft spot, waterfalling this golden energy out and about your human body all the way down to your toes.

~~~~~Exercise of Feeling Your Upper and Lower Circuits~~~~~

A wonderful exercise to integrate this is to go for a short walk. Allow your lower circuit to flow with each breath you take. The earth's energy is coming up through your feet and through your legs, mixing with your divine or upper circuit energy and dropping down your grounding cord. At the same time, with each inhalation you are drawing in your upper circuit of golden healing energy. As your body becomes familiar with both of these circuits, it celebrates! Both can be circulating at the same time! Just consider being on the phone, digesting your lunch and folding clothes at the same time. We multitask all the time. Our body is intimately familiar with multiple functions occurring. With these two circuits both in form and you sitting in the center of your head, *You* are in the moment! This is what we call *Present Time*. You are consciously running your energy.

When we begin these exercises in meditation we experience what are called growth periods. There may be parts of us that form *Resistance*. We come up with all the reasons not to

27

have or do this. GIFT yourself with five minutes a day *to be Present, Ground your body and Run your circuits*. Your body will thank you.

This will not include 10 minutes on each foot. A wise teacher in the early 70's encouraged us to take our foot reflex charts out with us as we sat in front of the television. He suggested that we do each foot, and if there was another person watching television with us, that we place the chart in the middle and do each other's feet! Sometimes this may lead to putting the television on mute or turning it off in favor of nice music. Enjoy giving to yourself or a loved one.

~~~~~~~~Are you Grounded???~~Prove It Exercise~~~~~~~~

If you have a willing partner, this little exercise will assist you in the experience of being and feeling grounded.

One of you will be the *pushee* and one will be the *pusher*. Stand and face each other with an arm's distance between you. One of you, the *pushee*, will stand in a comfortable, regular, just hanging out, relaxed position.

Your partner, the *pusher*, will close their eyes, anchor themselves, bring the earth's energy up through their feet and gently drop it down their grounding cord, ground, open their eyes and then ask permission to gently push you on the shoulders.

Notice how your body responds.

Now, you take a nice deep breath in and ground your body. Your partner, the *pusher,* will again ask permission to gently push you on the shoulders. *Now, how did your body respond and feel? Did you notice and feel any differences?*

Exchange places. Have your partner become the *pushee* and you become the *pusher.*

When you have completed this exchange, share with each other. How different did it feel being grounded from ungrounded when you were pushed on?

Have you given consideration to where these tools will fit into your life? Some might activate their tools while taking their shower as they rinse, wash, rinse, relax in the water, they ground, run their upper and lower circuits and plunk themselves, their Beings and attention, down into the center of their heads in their oh-so-comfortable chair. The shower folk find themselves in present time, taking their shower and clearing and balancing themselves at the same time.

Others may tie their tools to tasks they do each day. For some, grounding is connected to brushing their teeth. As they are brushing they are also breathing and allowing their lower circuit to activate!

Washing dishes, doing laundry, booting up your computer, whenever and wherever it fits into your life, gift yourself with the use of these tools you are gathering.

On that night so long ago that I first experienced calling back my energy, attention and focus, I was certain that my relationship with my boss would be improved. I never thought about Bill. Normally when I arrived home he would have been asleep for several hours. On this class night, he sat up in bed and asked, "What the dickens did you do in class tonight? I was sitting and watching Star Trek when all of a sudden I felt this whoosh of energy come and smack me." I bent over and kissed him and said, "We gave everyone back their energy, attention and focus. It never occurred to me that you would be in my space and I in yours??!!" I was young. I did however note to myself that I would put *roses*, described in Class Four, all around me on Saturday when he did his turn in class so that I didn't get whooshed!

With a nice deep breath in, remember your tool box or container. Gently place each of your newly gathered tools into this space.

You now have these tools available to you **any time, any place:**

1. Your own unique grounding cord, the ability to gently draw the earth's energy up through your feet and drop it down your grounding cord, thereby activating your lower circuit,

2. your unique sanctuary in the center of your head,

3. **gently** calling back all of your energy, attention and focus and filtering it down your upper circuit, allowing your life force energy to be returned to your body,

4. and breathing in your connection to your divine/higher self with the flow of your warm golden energy following your upper circuit.

Take a moment to consider, how and what, do you experience and feel when you are grounded. Take a deep breath in and know that you may do and have this **any time, any place**.

Class Three

**Balloons, Boundaries,
Your Space, My Space,
Roses, Emotion,
Sensing Your Aura,
Feel Your Aura**

A balloon is fun to have for learning this tool.

With ease now, please take in a nice deep breath. Gently exhale. Become aware of where you are sitting. Are you comfortable? Are your neck and lower back supported? Arrange yourself so that your human body is comfortable. Again, draw in a nice deep breath, allowing the earth's energy to come up through your feet as you inhale. As you exhale, gently allow the earth's current to drop down your grounding cord. Allow your grounding cord to expand to the width of your hips. Take in several of these nice deep breaths allowing your lower circuit to flow through you. Ahh.

Take notice of the center of your head--your room. Have you been there lately? This is a grand place to hang out during your day. This is your unique sanctuary. **One being to one body. Human Being.** This is your space. It is great to claim it each morning! Find your time. Brushing your teeth, taking your shower, doing your yoga stretches, making your family's lunches. **Any time and place** that fits for you!

Plunk your being down into that chair in the center of your head and look out your big picture windows at your world.

THIS IS YOUR PRESENT TIME.

This is where the *power* to effect change is. From this space in the center of your head you may direct your breath to any place in your body. Check your body. Is there any place that feels tight, anxious, or nervous...? Take a nice deep breath in and exhale your breath through that area. Allow it to relax. Use your breath to support your body in relaxing.

When your room feels comfortable to you, remember the tool of breathing with that warm golden energy from your higher or divine self. With a nice deep breath gently breathe in this warm golden energy. Bring it in through the top of your head, at your soft spot. Allow this current of your life force energy to travel down along the back of your spine as you inhale. A little drops down your grounding cord and then, as you exhale, bring this current up the front of your spinal column to your throat. Let it flow across your shoulders, down your arms to your hands. Once you feel your energy in your hands, allow it to come back up to your throat, flushing up across your face, washing your big picture windows and cascading out the top of your head over your body down to your toes.

Now call back your energy, attention and focus from all of the people, places and things where it was directed. With your filter above your head, sitting in the center of your head, gently call your energy, attention and focus back to your body. Breathe and feel your body replenish itself with your life force energy. This is a nice place to again say hello to your body. Is there any place that would like you to pay attention to it? Just breathe to the area, acknowledging that you have heard its request for your attention. This is your **being** listening to your **body** and responding to its request!

If you have been taking many deep breaths, your body is now oxygenated. Sometimes our eyes make tears when we do this. Sometimes we yawn. Both are wonderful physical signs that your energy is running and blockages are being dissolved. Another tool is to stretch your arms up as if you were climbing a ladder and then bending over to pat your legs. Uncurl your spine slowly, vertebra by vertebra, then slowly sit back up and check in with your body. How does it feel?

Congratulate yourself for giving yourself this time to read and experience your body and being in communication.

~Boundaries...Your Space...My Space...Balloons and Roses~

Pick up your balloon. Consider some one or thing that is irritating to you. Blow this image into your balloon as you fill it with air. When you have blown it as big as you wish, hold it up in the air and let go of it! It will fly around you, dispersing the hot air! If this causes you to laugh, do so! Again think of some irritant and blow your balloon up. Let it go flying all about you dispersing and releasing that irritating energy.

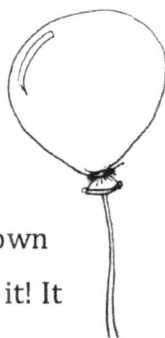

~~~~~~Roses~~~~~~

Sitting comfortably in your surroundings, gently close your eyes and look out of your picture windows. This is your being viewing outside of your body. Create an image of a rose. Look at its shape, color, size, length of stem, whether it has thorns or no thorns. Does it smell? Say hello to your ability to visualize. Gently let the rose evaporate, melt or dissipate, whatever suits you. This is the equivalent of the air dispersing out of the balloon.

A rose is a neutral image or symbol. There will be many uses for our roses. Imagine that you now have ONE MILLION roses at your disposal. If you use them all up, you will have another one million! You now have an *unending* supply.

~~~~~~~ Your Space, My Space ~~~~~~~

One use for your roses is to mark your boundary, your space. Visualize a picket fence with rose bushes along the outside. This is a marking of space. A rose may also be used as a decoy, magnet or filter for incoming energy. Say hello to the concept of and need for awareness of your space and my space.

Close your eyes and look around your room. This IS your space. Claim it. Now look outside your window and visualize a rose. If you find someone between you

36

and your rose, they are in your space. Say "Hello" to them in spirit and ask them to return to their own space. Sometimes this happens when someone we know is curious about what we are doing. They pop into our space to check us out. We all do it. So this is not a good or a bad thing. It is how we maneuver through life until we understand how energy works. Once we begin to understand and distinguish how my energy is in concert with me and your energy is in concert with you, we manage our energy with greater respect and wisdom.

When you are with one or more people you may place a rose between you and them. The rose will serve as a filter between you and the other person. You may walk into a meeting with a bouquet of imagined or imaged roses. One floats out between you and each of the other folks in the room. You now have filters surrounding you. Each of us has had an occasion when this would have proven to be quite useful.

The rose will also serve as a protection device, filtering any unwanted energy being directed your way. In the case of a meeting jealousy, rivalry, competition, fear for job security are all different forms of energy or emotion that may arise.

The American Heritage Dictionary defines *emotion* as "a strong feeling; a state of mental agitation or disturbance" and how about we add bliss and ecstasy.

Just as we filled our balloon with an irritant, we may now image a rose outside of our picture window. Consider for a moment something that annoys, creates anxiety or just plain irritates you. Allow it to be drawn into the rose. With a nice deep breath gently allow that rose to dissipate! What quality or feeling would you like to replace that irritant with? With a nice deep breath, breathe that into the space you just cleared.

All of your knowing and remembering,

your information, in-form-ation,

is inside of you.

Say "Hello" to your inner guidance.

Your energy is uniquely yours.

It is like your oil. Other folk's energy is like water in your oil or space. Give it back to them. And vice versa: your energy in their space is like water in their oil. We use the term oil for life force energy or CHI because of its lubricating qualities. Our life force energy, like oil, makes things flow with ease when it is within us.

My friend, Marylin says, "No harm or blame to you and no harm or blame to me, I gently call my energy back to me." We all know that the Power to effect change is available in any given moment.

We call it *Present Time.*

~~~~*One Use of Your Rose....Prove-It Exercise*~~~~

If you have a willing partner, agree to share a story with each other. Place the image of a rose between you and share a short story. Dissolve the rose and share another story. Exchange, so that you may experience hearing a story with your rose in place and one without a rose serving as a filter. Does it feel different? If so, how?

~~~~~~~*Exercise Feeling our CHI*~~~~~~~

Chi stance: stand on your feet with your hips and shoulders aligned. Breathe in and out. Feel your upper and lower circuits in motion.

~~~~~~~ *Sensing Your Aura* ~~~~~~~

This tool is used in sensing the aura. Imagine your electromagnetic field coming in to one and a half feet in front of you, along side you, in back of and next to you, above and below you. This is your universe. Breathe. Feel how your body responds to being surrounded by your electromagnetic field, your aura.

It is like the **being** in the center of your head has the **body**. Your **body** has your aura surrounding it. Own this, your space. Your energy, in your space, feels comfortable. Others' energy does not.

There now exist cameras that may photograph your aura. Aura Imaging Company in Redwood City has the Aura Camera 6000 and Aura Imaging Systems. Auras are perceived electronically, using a computer program to transform measured energy impulses into an auric image. You may find one of these cameras at your local book store, healing fair or healing center.

There are at least seven layers to our aura.

They correspond to the seven chakras or energy centers along our spine. You will experience more about your energy centers in Class Four.

Sitting in the center of your head, become aware of your aura. You first felt it at eighteen inches out. Bring it in to an extended elbow's distance from your body. This is handy when we get on an elevator and just want to have a little bit of space around us. With awareness from the center of your head, feel your grounding and your body. How do they feel with your aura in close? After a few moments, allow your aura to expand to three feet out. Stretch your arms out and let your aura be at this boundary all the way around you. Some sense this as an egg-shaped sphere an arm's length above our head, below our feet and out around us. A cocoon.

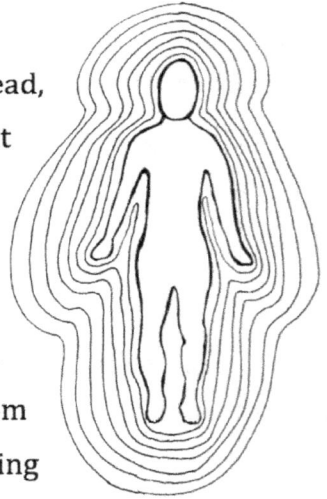

Above, below, next to and along side.

Feel this for some moments. What you will most likely discover is that it feels familiar. Your body has done this all along. Now you are conscious of it. Discover what your personal comfort distance is. It may be one distance at home, a different distance at work or play. And another distance at the dentist, doctor, standing in the grocery or post office line. Check it out.

We have used our auras forever. When we are preparing to walk into an unknown situation we project our aura out in front of us to check out the environment we are walking into.

We have all been in a room when we felt something from behind. We turn to look and take note of the someone *entering* the room. That person had their aura projected out in front of them and we felt or sensed it.

On the other hand, most of us have experienced being in an elevator. We start out with just this much space around us. Consider how much space this is for you. As more people board the elevator, we gently draw our auras in closer around us. What we want is just enough space so that we are not touching. Again, our bodies have been doing this for us all along. Acknowledge and validate this with and to your body.

Auras are used to sense physical, emotional and social guidelines. This energy field screens the environment we are entering and adjusts our energy centers accordingly.

~~~~~~~Feel Your Aura...Experience It Exercise~~~~~~~

Exercise: If you have a friend or companion who will read and do this with you, it is enjoyable to practice feeling each other's auras. As we did with *pushee/pusher* one will sit in a chair and gently bring their aura in around them to a comfortable distance. They may close their eyes to focus on what they are experiencing. The standing person will take a step or two away, gently ground and center themselves, running their lower and upper circuit and feeling their life force energy flow out of their hands. You will keep your eyes open. You don't want to poke them. Secondly you want to sense this from the center of your head, your space, not theirs.

When the person standing is in *present time*, they ask the person sitting, "May I feel your aura?" With your hands extended in front of you gently approach your sitting friend and sense where you feel the edge of their aura. Start up above and **out** from their head. Usually you are several feet away from your partner's body when your hands feel something. What is it? It is your partner's electromagnetic field, their aura. With your hands held open, gently sense, as you sweep along its boundaries, down their front, feeling how far out their aura is. Sometimes you sense color, temperature or feelings from your partner.

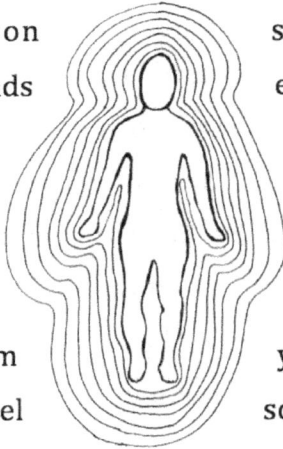

42

There are many ways to experience how this feels, so just be open to how you experience it. Move slowly around their body, feeling where their aura or boundary is. As you bring your hands to the back of where they are sitting, does your sense of their aura change? How? Sometimes the aura is out in front or behind the body. We want the body to be in the center of its aura. As you move down toward their hips and legs, is it the same distance out as it was up by their head and heart? There is no right or wrong to this. What you are experiencing is how your friend's aura is at this moment. It could change in an instant if someone else entered the room or if the phone rang. Our electromagnetic fields are in constant flux, adjusting to our environment. When you are done, gently shake your hands. This gently releases any energy you may have collected.

Exchange places and repeat this process. After you have both sat in the chair and experienced having your aura felt, share with each other how it was. Differentiate the sensation of feeling the aura from the sitting in the chair having your aura felt.

When I took these classes, we were given homework. We were asked to practice and briefly share what we experienced while using our newfound tools in class the following week.

This particular class left me with a set of lessons that would stay with me for decades. When Bill finished his class on Saturday, we agreed to meet up in San Francisco to check out elevators. I brought our daughters up to meet him and we boarded a cable car on the corner of Market and Union Streets in San

Francisco. We each took a seat. As we moved along the line, more people boarded at each stop. Finally two elderly women climbed on with their grocery bags. Bill and I stood for them to sit on either side of our daughters. As more people boarded standing room became congested. I was holding the upper hand rail as I felt a body lean up and into mine. My eyes widened as I looked across the seat to where Bill was standing. His eyes were on fire as he prepared to move toward me. I flashed him a "Wait just a minute!" I took a deep breath and moved my aura out in back of me and then all around me. As the energy from my aura moved out behind me, so did the man who had pressed up against me. He had a strange look on his face according to Bill. He disembarked at the next stop. Bill and I pondered, "Was it really that easy?"

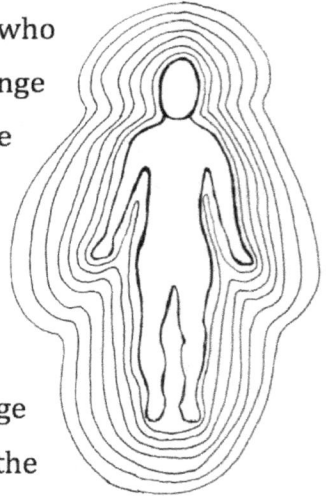

When we arrived home to Moss Beach, our friend and neighbor called and asked if we would like backstage tickets to the Rolling Stones concert for the next day at Candlestick Park. I told her that I would ask Bill. I had college homework and felt the afternoon had been spent playing in the City. Bill looked at me as if I were askew. Of course, we would like tickets to see the Rolling Stones! I called my friend back and said of course and thank you.

The next day I found myself backstage on a platform set up to house the Rolling Stones before they went out on their stage.

Each of them had their own room. The fans had begun to chant and stomp their feet. The very ground beneath us was rumbling and the air was vibrating with Mick, Mick, Mick...One by one, the drummer and guitarists walked by us, rounded the corner onto the stage to huge explosions of sound from the field. It was a sold-out crowd. A door opened and a small wiry man exited, kind of running in place, slowly moving forward past us he began doing jumping jacks. It was the one of the darndest things I had ever experienced as my vision shifted and I saw his aura growing, expanding out in front of him. As Mick Jagger moved around the bend where the crowd caught their first glimpse of him, he was moving his aura out in front of himself. When he grabbed the microphone he had expanded his aura out to include the whole of Candlestick Park. And, oh my, my, how loud it became, with the music, huge speakers, and a crowd of 50,000 people yelling in delight.

My teacher noted in class the following week how I had been gifted with two very distinct experiences of aura. Yes we could expand our auras out as big and wide as a baseball park. As it turns out, with ease, in fact. The trick is to know how to bring it back in around you. Our teacher pointed out that many famous rock and roll musicians, as well as prominent people in politics, science and medicine all were able to expand their auras to engage their audiences. What many had not learned to do was to *bring their auras back in around them at the end*. They used drugs

45

or alcohol to close down their energy systems. We saw many examples of this in this era.

In the early 1980's, teachers were brought in to some of Silicon Valley's well known companies to provide workshops to the top sales people. Global markets and very big money was at stake. These companies could not afford the drug or alcohol use by their top sales people, before or after their presentations. Whether it was named stress reduction or body awareness or whatever, the art of centering, clearing and focusing were tools that could and would be appreciated in the sales workforce.

Becoming aware of your aura and where it is about you may feel empowering. It allows you conscious choice of how and where you want your boundaries to be.

With a nice deep breath in, remember your toolbox or container. Gently place each of your newly gathered tools into this space.

You now have available to you **any time, any place** the following tools:

1. Your own unique grounding cord, the ability to gently draw the earth's energy up through your feet and drop it down your grounding cord, thereby activating your lower circuit,

2. the center of your head, one being to one body, your unique sanctuary,

3. the ability to call back all of your energy, attention and focus from where you have spread it out through your day, filtering your life force energy down your upper circuit and allowing your life force energy to be returned to your body,

4. breathing in your connection to your divine/higher self with your flow of warm, golden healing energy along your upper circuit,

5. the ability to use a balloon or rose as a decoy or filter,

6. doing the CHI stance ,

7. and the ability to draw or expand your aura, electromagnetic field, in around, above and below you **any time, any place**.

With a nice deep breath just allow the feeling and knowing that you have gathered all of these tools into your space for your use.

47

Class Four

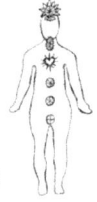

Aura Cleansing Exercise, Roses, Primary Chakras, one through seven and Protection

As I teach these classes I marvel at this, the half-way mark and the number of empowering tools we have gathered already. When I took the classes, they were one through six. Meditation Two was class seven through twelve. I was so taken with class seven, that, I thought if I were ever to teach these classes I would include cords in Meditation One. The reason was that if no further classes were taken this tool would be available.

At this point you have gathered many tools into your space. Congratulate yourself.

You have grounding, the center of your head, your lower circuits and your upper circuits, calling back all of your energy, attention and focus and filtering your life force energy along your upper circuit, roses as filters and bringing your own unique electromagnetic field or aura in around you. Your tool chests/ containers are filling up.

Take a nice deep breath in. *Validate* that each of these tools is in your container. Feel your body as you complete this review. Say hello to your being plunking down in that chair in the center of your head. As you look out of your big picture windows, acknowledge where you are right now. This is your space and you claim it! However it is, just say hello and acknowledge it.

Mindfulness "is attentive and heedful, thorough and cautious." These are tools you now have at your disposal, **any time, any place**. Remember when you last used them. Consider when it may have been of service to you to use them.

~~~~~~~~Aura Cleansing Exercise~~~~~~~~

As an exercise, identify where your aura is around you now. Is it close in or spread way out about you? As you become aware of its edges, consider unzipping it, shaking it out and putting it back around you, zipping it back up. Use nice slow deep breaths as you do this.

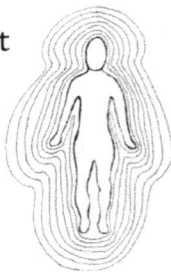

I often use the wind to assist me in this. When I find myself in a blustery environment I gently let my aura expand and the gusts of wind blow through, clearing and cleaning it with air. Then with a nice deep breath in, I pull my aura back in around my body to a comfortable distance for my present time.

~~~~~~~~Roses~~~~~~~~

Roses have so *many* uses.

One is a protection device. The rose may serve as a decoy at the edge of your aura. Energy coming at you is met by your rose and deflected down its stem into the earth. Your being remains comfortable in the center of your head. Your body remains at ease with your aura in around it, surrounded by your roses.

With your aura comfortably about you and a rose in front of you, along one side of you, behind you and along your other side, all serving as filters of incoming energy, how do you feel in your space? Just take several nice, slow, deep breaths and feel this space your body is in.

With a nice deep breath, sitting in the center of your head, looking out of your picture windows, imagine being with your best friend, love, mother or sibling. Where do you sense your aura when you are with these different folks?

If you need to, put a rose down between you and that other person. Do you feel the difference when you define your space? Are you able to view these other folks without becoming involved or remaining neutral? Are you able to sense your aura and theirs? If this makes you uncomfortable, take a nice deep breath, move the discomfort out into a rose in front of your big picture windows and let it go; dissolve it. Gently call back your energy attention and focus.

~~~~~~~~Chakras~~~~~~~~

CHAKRAS are another name for the energy centers found along our spine. The word Chakra means wheel in Sanskrit. There are seven primary chakras located from the base of the spine to the top of our heads. We also have smaller energy centers located in our hands, feet and throughout our bodies where some of our meridian

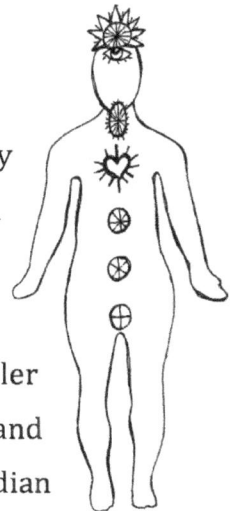

lines cross. If you are familiar with acupuncture, this is where they might place the needles.

Chakras are more commonly understood in the Eastern traditions, both medical and spiritual. Consider the lotus flower. For some this is a representation of the chakra opening, closing and spinning as we move through our day.

~~~~~~~~Location of our Primary Chakras~~~~~~~~

Our first chakra is located at the base of our spine. This is where our sitz bone, coccyx or tailbone is. Our first chakra is connected to the element of Earth; our survival: food, clothing and shelter. It is sometimes referred to as our root chakra.

Our second chakra resides between our pelvic bones, and the ovaries or vas deferens tubes. Our second chakra is connected to the element of Water; our sexuality, sensuality, balance, creativity, a healthful distribution of our vitality.

Our third chakra is located at the base of our sternum. It is where we do the Heimlich maneuver, the maneuver used when someone is choking to dislodge any objects in throat. In the martial arts it is called the Ka point. Our third chakra is connected to the element of Fire; our individual will power, gut instincts, our ability to manifest in to physical form.

Our fourth chakra resides along our heart center. Our fourth chakra is our center for compassion, unconditional love and connection with our divine. This is our balancing chakra. Our lower three chakras are body based. Our upper three chakras are

Being based. Our heart is our center for balancing our body and being. The fulcrum on a teeter- totter.

Our fifth chakra is located at our throat. This chakra is our grand central station. It is home to our communication, both through our voice and our hands. This fifth chakra is where we express ourselves, our will, say yes, say no, ask for help and speak our truth.

Our sixth chakra is located at the center of our heads. Imagine that. It is where our room is in the center of our heads. Our sixth chakra is where our clear seeing resides along with our ability for ESP, extra sensory perception, psychic abilities, dissolution of karma and healing ourselves.

Our seventh chakra is located at the top of our heads. It is sometimes called our crown chakra. It is where our soft spot was when we were born. Our seventh chakra is where we connect to our higher selves, Unity and liberation.

As you reread where each of these chakras are, place one of your hands where it is located. Sense this location on your body. Where would it be on the back side of you? A chakra has a front and a back opening along your spine. If we were to look at a chakra it would appear as a spinning vortex or a lotus flower, opening and closing, pulsing as you move through your day. Your body has been familiar with your chakras all along. If you are just learning about them it is your mind that is just now meeting them.

We have all encountered someone who had a love encounter over the weekend. We see them on a foggy Monday morning and they are telling us what a beautiful day it is. We can feel exuberance and love emanating from them. Their heart chakra is wide open and pulsing rapidly.

Eeyore drawn by M. McEachen

Then we see them at a later date on a sunny day. They are in full Eeyore form (the wonderful donkey in the Winnie the Pooh stories), grumping about the day. Their heart chakra is pulsing slowly.

We also have encountered those folks who always seem to feel grounded, safe to be near, rocks of Gibraltar. Their first chakra is balanced and they are grounded.

There are whole books written about our energy centers, our chakras. A local national bookstore had 147 books with information on chakras. On the web there are many sites that may be resourced. For our purposes we are going to feel each one and get to know its location on our bodies.

With a nice deep breath, feel your warm, golden upper circuit begin to flow down your spine and up the front of your spine to your throat, down your arms to your hands, back up your arms, across the front of your face and up and out of the top of your head.

We are actually flushing our energy through our palm chakras or energy centers. Just as our feet have chakras in them, so do the palms of our hands. With your eyes comfortably closed, sitting in the center of your head, you will take seven or more nice deep breaths in, gently "exhaling" through each of your chakras one at a time. You may have a hand placed in front and one behind each chakra as you sense it. STAY in the center of your head, observe with neutrality as you do this.

Use your hands to feel the chakra. Is it wide open, closed down, pulsing, any particular temperature or color? Is the front the same as the back? Most of us seem to have the front of our chakras a bit more open than the back.

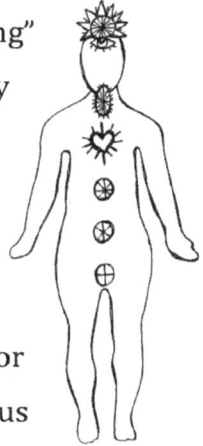

For some folks it will be difficult to use their hands to feel their chakras. It may be easier for them to sit with their eyes closed and look at an image of their body turned sideways outside of their picture windows. As you consider each of your chakras, beginning with your first, notice how the chakra looks. Is it wide open or shut down to a trickle? Is the front the same as the back? Any sense of temperature or color?

When you have reviewed each of your chakras you may want to note your experience of them. Draw your chakras on your body picture on page 19.

55

Let us consider now when we bring our aura in around us that we place seven roses at its edge in front of us, parallel to each of our chakras, seven roses behind us, parallel to each of our chakras, and one rose on either side of us. The rose on either side of us acts as a filter for any energy coming at us from the side. The rose is parallel to our head with a stem traveling down along the edge of our aura. The energy hits the rose and travels down the stem to the earth to be grounded off. As we engage with life, energy comes to us from the front and behind.

Our chakras are protected by our auric field and these roses serve as filters for incoming energy.

Good thing we have a million roses at our disposal and that if we use them all up we receive a million more!

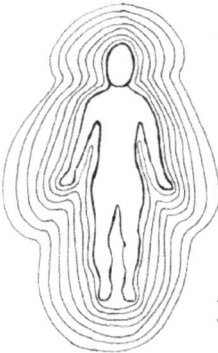

~~~~~~~~Review~~~~~~~~

To review our tools, consider your ability to gently call your aura in around you. Allow seven roses to take form in front and back of your seven chakras. Allow a rose to take form on either side of you. With a nice deep breath, have a clear sense of the center of your head. This is your space and you have claimed it. Take a look around your room. Any one

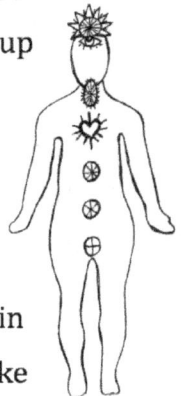

else in here with you, say "Hello", go outside or to the center of your own head. This is my space. My sanctuary, my command central.

One being to one body or my being in my body!

With a nice deep breath, gently draw the earth's energy up through your foot chakras or energy centers, up along your calves and thighs to the base of your spine or your first chakra. Allow your grounding cord to be as wide as your hips and exhale down your grounding cord. Down your grounding cord goes, to the center of the earth, connecting, anchoring you.

With your being firmly in your chair in the center of your head, you may call back all of your energy, attention and focus. Allow it to come in through your filter above your head, into your seventh or crown chakra, flowing down along the back of your spinal column. As it gets to the back side of your sixth chakra, let it flow out to your aura. You will move your life force energy through the back of each of your chakras as you do this inhalation. With ease, just let it flush through the back of your fifth chakra, throat; your fourth chakra, heart; your third chakra, solar plexus; your second chakra, between your pelvic bones and at your first chakra at the base of your spine, flushing out into your aura. As you exhale, bring this, your life force energy, up your spine, through the front of your first, second, third, fourth, fifth, sixth and seventh chakras.

Now you have replenished your body's energy centers, chakras, with your life force energy. Take another breath and draw in your warm golden healing energy from your higher self. Allow it to follow this same upper circuit with a gentle flush through each of your chakras beginning at the back of the seventh. Allow the golden energy to flush through the back of your seventh chakra, clearing, stabilizing and healing this energy center and taking any residue out to your rose to be discarded down its stem. As you continue this inhalation, your golden healing energy flows through your sixth chakra, clearing, stabilizing and healing this energy center, taking any residue out to your rose for disposal. Continue with this inhalation, clearing, stabilizing and healing the back of your fifth, fourth, third, second and first chakras. Obviously, the first few times it takes more than one breath. What happens though is that the body becomes familiar with this motion and will learn to do it in one graceful inhalation of your golden healing energy from your higher self.

It is the same with the exhalation on the front of the spinal column. We exhale this warm golden healing energy from our higher divine self through our first chakra, allowing any residue to go out to our rose for disposal. We allow some of this golden healing energy riding our exhalation to move through our second chakra, clearing, stabilizing and healing it, with any residue moving out to our rose for disposal. We move this energy up and out through all seven of our chakras on our exhalation. When we arrive at our seventh chakra, we allow this golden healing energy to waterfall out over our bodies to our toes and out into our aura.

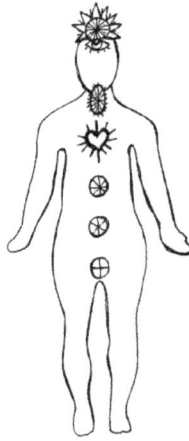

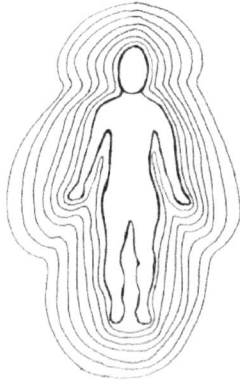

Illustrations by Chayo Wilson

With a nice deep breath in, remember your toolbox or container. Gently place each of your newly gathered tools along side those you already hold in your space:

1. Grounding,
2. running your lower and upper circuits,
3. your aura,
4. roses,
5. the center of your head,
6. clearing out and running your own healing energy through your chakras
7. calling back your energy, attention and focus.

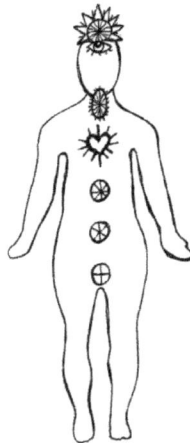

Class Five

Emotions, Exercise in Blowing Roses, Playing with Energy

Consider the tools you have collected so far. With a nice deep breath, gently draw the earth's energy up through the arches of your feet, (this is the location of your primary foot chakra), up along your calves and thighs, up to the base of your spine. With a gentle exhalation allow this earth energy to drop down your grounding cord, which is as wide as your hips, to the center of the earth. Your lower circuit is now in motion. Take note of the ease in which you did this.

With your next nice, deep breath, have a sense of the center of your head. This is your space and you claim it.

One Being to one Body.

If there is any one else in your room, say, "Hello; go outside to the center of your own head. This is my unique sanctuary." Take a look around your room. Is it all you could ask for and have? If not, adjust it! You are in charge here. You may have it any way you desire. It is your space, at your disposal, to create uniquely for yourself. Plunk or set your being into your chair at command central.

With a gentle breath, bring your aura in around you, above and below you. Feel your body surrounded by its electromagnetic

61

field, your aura. Ahh… From the center of your head, gently become aware of your seven energy centers or chakras. Allow a rose to take form parallel to the front and back of each of your chakras. Place a rose on either side of you at the edge of your aura.

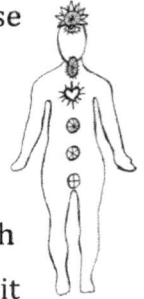

Place your filter above your head and call back your life force energy. Allow it to come in through the top of your head, replenishing the front of your seventh chakra. As it moves down the front of your forehead it replenishes the front of your sixth chakra. Continuing down to your throat it replenishes your fifth chakra, moving your energy out along your shoulders down your arms to your hands. Ahh. Your energy, attention and focus, your life force energy continue the flow down the front of your spine to your heart, replenishing your fourth chakra or energy center. Flowing down the front of your spine, you arrive at your third chakra, your solar plexus, and allow this energy center to be replenished. Continuing, you arrive at your second chakra, energy center, between your pelvic bones, and replenish this with your life force energy. At the end of this inhalation you arrive at your first chakra, at the base of your spine, and you gently allow it to be replenished with your life force energy.

As you exhale, your life force energy flows up through the front of your first chakra, then the second, third, fourth, fifth, sixth, with free window-washing, and up to your seventh at the top of your head, waterfalling out over your body down to your toes and out into your auric field.

With another gentle breath draw in your upper circuit from your higher, divine self. Allow this exquisite, golden, healing energy to come in at the top of your head and flow down along the back of your spinal column, clearing, stabilizing and healing each of your chakras. Any residue is released out to your roses at the edge of your aura and flushed down their stems into the earth. As you exhale you move this golden, healing energy up the front of your spinal column flushing the fronts of your chakras. Again when you reach your seventh chakra, allow this golden energy to flow out into your auric field.

You are now in *Present Time*.

Feel what it is like in your body. Your energy centers have been flushed and replenished. It seems like so much to do when it is outlined in step-by-step wording like this. Find a time and place where this fits into your life. Some of those mundane tasks we do each and every day will hold the time.

Practice *Present Time* while brushing your teeth, taking your constitutional, your shower or bath, washing dishes or making coffee or tea, unlocking your door and putting your key into your ignition.

NOTE: The one place I have been encouraged not to do this is when I am actually driving my vehicle. Obviously, closing my eyes and activating my upper and lower circuits is not wise! While stopped at a light, confirming I am present in the center of my head is fine. We do shift a gear when we meditate. A part of our focus will not be present in our mundane experience.

All of these acts, from brushing your teeth to placing your key in your ignition, hold time and space for you to incorporate your tools. Gift yourself with the regular time and place or space to use these tools you are accumulating.

~~~~~~~~~~~~~~Emotions~~~~~~~~~~~~~~~

Emotions are the **Body's** communication to the **Being** or our spirit. Emotion = *Energy in Motion.* As you feel these different emotions, you will have the opportunity to let go of that which you are ready to release, that which no longer serves your highest well being. Allow some roses to take form at the edge of your aura. If you have any feelings of doubt, guilt, or "I can't do this stuff," send them to the roses and allow them to disintegrate. These are no longer truths in your space.

Allow a rose to take form at the edge of your aura and looking out of your big picture windows, send any feelings of doubt or *less than* "<" to the rose. Allow the rose to disintegrate and then call back your energy, attention and focus. Replace that doubt or sense of *less than* with confidence, your highest well being, love, light, or whatever suits you.

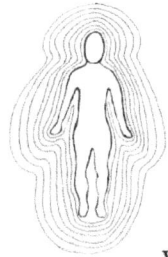

~~~~~~~Playing with Energy~~~~~~~

We will imagine a wonderful cloak rack with seven cloaks arranged out in front of our aura. Allow a wonderful mirror to take form in your room. You will be able to view these emotions on your mirror. When you are ready you will gently reach out and wrap yourself in cloak number one.

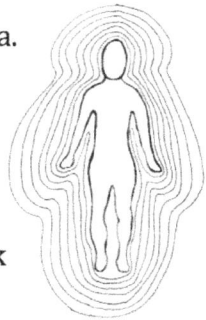

Feel the emotion of apathy. *Apathy* is defined as "lack of interest or concern in important matters."

Look into the mirror in the center of your head. Sense yourself wrapped in the cloak of apathy. Feel your body. Is it in communication with your being? Remember the last time you felt apathy. How well can you function in apathy? How do you feel? What can you create and/or engage in from the emotion of apathy? How is your grounding when you are in apathy? How much energy can you have when you are in apathy? Are you empowered in apathy? Whew! With a nice deep breath, take the cloak of apathy off and move it out into a rose or balloon at the edge of your aura. Let it go, dissipate. Take a nice deep breath in. Feel yourself in the center of your sanctuary in *present time*. Those emotions sure shift our gears, huh? Breathe.

Feel your body come back to your place of center.

Reach up for cloak number two and look into your mirror in the center of your head. Wrap your aura in the emotion of Boredom. *Boredom* is defined as "To make weary by being dull, repetitive or tedious".

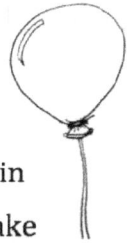

Remember the last time you felt boredom.

How well are you able to function when you are bored? How do you feel when you are bored? How well do you engage or create when you are in the emotion of boredom? How is your grounding? How much energy do you experience when you are in boredom? Are you empowered? With a nice deep breath, gently release this cloak of boredom. Move it out of your aura into a rose or balloon and release it. Breathe and return to your place of center, present time.

A note on Boredom straight from my notes from Karen's class states,

"We may experience *boredom* when we are not in *present time*. Our thoughts are in the past or future not in the moment. Our *being* becomes bored with not being present in our life experience. When we are present there is so much input that there is no possible way we could be bored."

When you are comfortable in your body and ready, look into your mirror, take in your nice deep breath and reach up for cloak number three. Bring the emotion of amusement in around you. *Amusement* is defined as "To cause to laugh."

Feel your body. Is it in communication with your Being? Remember the last time you felt amusement. How well do you function when you are in amusement? What can you engage in and create when you are in the emotion of amusement? How is your grounding when you are in amusement? How much energy can you have when you are in amusement? Are you empowered in amusement? How well can you hear, smell, feel? Breathe. Feel how this feels to your body and your being. When you are ready, take a nice deep breath in and gently take off the cloak of amusement. Move it out into a rose or balloon at the edge of your aura and allow it to dissipate. Take another nice deep breath in. Feel yourself in the center of your sanctuary in *present time*. Feel your body come back to its position of center.

When you are comfortable in your body and ready, look into your mirror, take in your nice deep breath and reach up for cloak number four. Bring the emotion of guilt in around you. *Guilt*

67

is defined as: "Remorseful awareness of having done something wrong; self reproach."

Remember the last time you felt guilty. How well do you function when you are feeling guilty? How well do you interact, create and engage when you are in the emotion of guilt? How is your grounding? How do you experience your energy when you are feeling guilty? Are you empowered? With a nice deep breath, gently release this cloak of guilt. Move it out of your aura into a rose or balloon and release it. Call back your energy, attention and focus and allow your body to return to present time.

As you find yourself comfortable within and without, continue to just breathe in and out several more times. Most of us find many pictures or memories stored with each of these emotions. You are releasing some of these when you move the cloak of emotion out into your rose to dissipate. When you feel at ease, look in the mirror and gently reach up for cloak number five.

Bring the emotion of anger in around you. *Anger* is defined as, "Displeasure, hostility, resentment, threatening, inflamed, painful." Remember the last time you felt angry.

How well do you function when you are feeling angry? How is your grounding? How is your energy when you are in a state of anger? What can you engage in and create from the emotion of anger? Are you empowered when you are angry?

With a nice deep breath, take the cloak of anger off and release it out into a rose and dissipate it. Take several more nice deep breaths. Use your roses to release more if you wish or need

68

to. Call back your energy, attention and focus. Allow yourself to come into present time.

As you feel yourself in present time, your being and body centered, remember how emotions come and go as you move through your day. An event, person, place or thing triggers a response. You experience an emotion.

Only two cloaks left.

When you feel ready, look into your mirror and reach out for cloak number six. Wrap your aura with the emotion of resistance. *Resistance* is defined as, "A force that opposes or retards motion; to strive or work against."

Remember the last time you felt resistance. I don't want to. I don't have to. How well do you function when you are in resistance? How is your grounding? How is your energy flowing when you are in resistance? Are you empowered when you are in resistance? What can you engage in and create when you are in resistance?

With a gentle cleansing breath, gently release this cloak of resistance into a rose. Dissipate it. Call back your energy, attention and focus. Breathe in your delicious golden healing energy from your higher and divine self. Look up at your rack: only one cloak left to try on, for now.

When you are comfortable, look into your mirror as you gently reach up for cloak number seven and wrap it around your aura. Remember the last time you felt the emotion of joy. *Joy* is defined as, "Intense or elated happiness. A source of great pleasure."

How well do you function when you are in joy? How is your grounding? How is your energy flowing? How well can you hear or smell? What can you engage in and create when you are in the emotion of joy? Are you empowered when you are in joy?

When you are ready, gently release this emotion of joy. Allow the cloak, cloak rack and mirror to move into a rose and be released. Call back your energy, attention and focus. Breathe in and out.

This may be a nice time to gently reach up over your head and stretch. Bend over and let your fingers and hands gently tap your feet or legs as you slowly uncurl your spine back up into a sitting position.

Envision being grounded, present in the center of your head, your aura in around you, your roses in place, your life force energy in you.

Own your space. This is your universe. Ahh.

Consider that when you find yourself in the midst of any negative or uncomfortable emotion, you have the power and choice to take that cloak of emotion off and release it. To the contrary, if you find yourself cloaked in amusement or joy or any of the other emotions that put a smile on your face, you may hang out in it. Feel it, luxuriate in it. You can practice feeling emotions with this tool. Play with it at your leisure. Use your roses to release the energy or pictures that come up on your mirror that no longer feel comfortable in your space. Call back your life force energy. Place your golden energy into these spaces.

Consider which of these emotions were familiar? Which did you like least? Which did you like most? You get to decide how do you want to feel, by choosing which cloak of emotion you will wear or take off? This is a grand tool to add to your toolbox.

With a nice deep breath in, remember your container or toolbox.

1. Gently place the art of experiencing an emotion, feeling it, taking it on and off, into your container,

2. along with your expanded ability to breathe your life force energy through each of your seven chakras in the art of a breath in and a breath out and

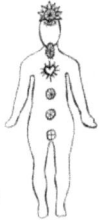

3. your golden healing energy, from your higher/ divine self, through each of your chakras in the art of a breath in and breath out.

4. Both are following your upper circuit.

5. Bring your aura in around, above and below you

6. with seven roses at its edge in front and back of your chakras,

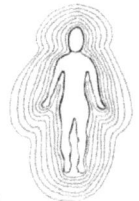

7. Create your lower circuit, breathing the earth's energy up through your foot chakras, along your legs and dropping it down your grounding cord, which is as wide as your hips and

8. sitting so comfortably in the center of your head, your unique sanctuary one being in one body, and your being in your body!

Congratulate yourself for gathering all these tools into your space for your use.

Class Six

Colors,
Blowing more Roses,
Exercise in Havingness And Why
Meditate

As you begin with this class, validate yourself for taking your time and energy to gather these tools for yourself. With a nice deep breath you now are able to draw the earth's energy up to your first chakra and drop it down as you exhale. With your next nice deep breath, you plunk your **Being** down into its chair in the center of your head and take a look around your command central. If you ever find anyone else in your room with you a cheery, "Hello; go outside; this is my space", is appropriate. One **being** to one **body**. This Is Your Space and You Claim It!

With your next nice deep breath in, gently call your aura in around, next to, above and below you. Sense your boundaries; where it ends. Now your body has its electromagnetic field in around it. With a breath in, allow your filters or roses to take form parallel to each of your seven chakras, at the front and back edge of your aura and one on either side.

With your next nice deep breath in allow your filter to take form above your seventh chakra and gently call back all of your energy, attention and focus from all the people places and things you have engaged with. With your next nice deep breath, inhale gently and allow your life force energy to pass through your filter

73

and come in at the top of your seventh chakra. Allow this, your life force energy, to travel down the back of your spine, moving out through the back of each of your chakras, as you inhale. At the base of your spine, with your exhalation gently continue your life force energy path up the front of your spinal column, flushing each of your seven chakras on its way up.

With your next nice deep breath in gently sense your higher and divine self and draw in your warm golden healing energy following this same upper circuit. You flush each of your seven energy centers with your golden healing energy. Your chakras are cleared out, stabilized and healed. Any residue is dispersed out into the roses at the edge of your aura, dropped down their stems and grounded into the earth.

You, **body** and **being** are now in Present Time. Take another nice deep breath in and slowly exhale. Say hello to your Present Time.

~~~~~~~~~~~~~Colors~~~~~~~~~~~~~

This exercise is to experience how colors feel to our mind and body. With your body in a comfortable sitting position, feet flat on the floor, comfortable in the center of your head, imagine a box with many pint containers of water-based paint. Slowly reach in for your first pint. Pour it over you and consider the following questions with each color.

Do you like this color surrounding you?

How does your body feel surrounded in this color?

Does it feel warm, cold or neutral?

Do you feel it more on your right or left side?

Where does the color want to go?

Try on each of the following colors: red, orange or peach, sunshine yellow, emerald green, brown mud earth, sky blue, violet and indigo.

Imagine a giant shower that rinses the color off of you and out of your aura, draining it down your grounding cord. Make the sound ahhhh for as long as a breath lasts as you wash each color off. My friend, Chayo notes that she loves taking a shower in the glow of each color, letting it tune her space and leaving some of the color in the spaces that want it. Suit yourself.

After trying on the above eight colors, you might try on white, briefly. There are times when the color white stirs up memories of being born in hospitals, medical establishments, confusion/purity, master/slave or guru/follower, so just be mindful when you try on white.

As we may feel different colors and shades resonate at different frequencies. We may enjoy more or less of a color at different times.

Lastly, choose the most divine and luxuriate in your shade of gold. Check out how it feels and then shower it off or leave it.

With a nice deep breath, close your eyes and see a meadow of your design with you in the center. Call to your high self to be present with you. Feel for a moment how this feels. Say hello to your abilities and the tools you have gathered unto yourself.

Roses are multifunctional. One use for a rose is to release and replace. With your feet flat on the floor, take a nice deep breath in and image a rose out in front of your big picture window at the edge of your aura. Consider a fear you hold within. Send the fear from where it resides in your body to the rose. Feel the contraction. We contract to protect ourselves from imagined loss before it even occurs. Release or dissipate the rose. Make another rose and fill it with what you would like to replace the fear with. It may be love, passion or your life force energy, whatever you choose. Gently bring that rose into your auric field and allow it to fill in the nooks and crannies that previously held your fear. Feel the expansion. Take in several slow breaths and feel your body adjust to the releasing and replacing of a fear.

With another rose at the edge of your aura, outside of your big picture windows, consider a belief that is no longer of service to you. As you release the belief into your rose, allow the memory of where it came from to go with it. No judgment. Using your breath, just release it into the rose. What do you want to replace this belief with? As you update your belief in accordance with you in present time allow this information to move through your body, filling the vacuum created by the release of the belief that is no longer of service to you.

You may clear and update your fears and beliefs at your leisure with these tools.

Reflecting back to bringing your aura in around you and how that may occur with ease now, consider your place of living. Sitting in the center of your head, create an image of your place of living outside your picture window. Gently bring the aura in front, either side, back, above and below of your place of living. If land surrounds you, include it. If you are on the fifteenth floor with ten other units, focus in on yours.

Gently bring the aura in around your living space and put roses on each of the boundaries. Some like to use the directions.

Bring the aura in from the East, South, West, North, above and below.

Imagine roses in all these places.

As with our living space, we may also use this tool with our vehicles. As we open our vehicle door or put our key into the ignition, we may gently bring the aura in around the vehicle, above and below it. We may draw the earth's energy up into the tires and drop it down a grounding cord as big as the vehicle if we'd like.

We are making the spaces we place our bodies in safe and sacred. In our culture we unconsciously get up and go out into our day. We exchange energy all through the day and it is no wonder that we are depleted as we head for home. It is an irony. For most of us, the reason we engage in work is to support our selves, families and home. If we expend most of our life force out and about in our work-a-day world, then the very people and reasons why we have engaged out in this world receive the dregs we have left over at the end of our day.

When we use the tools of staying in *Present Time* and calling back our energy attention and focus when we commute our way home, we are rejuvenating our bodies with our life force energy. When we place our bodies in a car that is grounded and has its aura in about it, we are creating a safe space for our body to relax in. To breathe in. This does not mean that the commute is not there. It is how we engage with the commute that is important.

It is the same with our places of living. To come home to a safe and sacred space allows our body to relax. With our energy, attention and focus replenishing us we are able to engage from a place of *Present Time* rather than a place of exhaustion and distraction.

When we arrive home to the very ones we love, if we are frazzled, worn and spent, there is not much joy in sharing time and space with us. However, when we make use of our tools we find that we have replenished our energy systems. We are enabled to interact and engage from a healthier more loving place.

~~~~~~~~~~~~***Exercise in Havingness*** ~~~~~~~~~~~~

With a nice deep breath, sitting comfortably, feet flat on the floor, from the center of your head look around your room. When it is absolutely comfortable, look out of your picture window. Consider: how would I live my life if there were nothing for me to worry about? Allow your body and being to receive that knowing with gentle slow deep breaths in and out.

At some point in your reflection, state,

"I am worthy. I will have..."

Simply, without thinking and engaging your internal dialogue. Were you surprised by what you could or could not have?

Gently breathe in and out. When you feel complete, open your eyes, stretch up and bend over and pat your body and then slowly uncurl your spine back up into a sitting position.

You are a being in your body for this lifetime. Own this truth.

Why might one want to meditate?

Your body already knows.

Give it permission to hear your own inner wisdom.

Feel your connection to the energy around you and then out and about you. Consider the tool of clearing and healing your energy centers by breathing your life force energy through them. When you are doing this you are clearing out, or releasing, other folk's energy that was in your space. Their water in your oil.

With your tools accessible and available to you **any time any place** your body will remember to take a nice deep breath. You are able to engage in ordinary experiences with a meditative view.

With a nice deep breath in, remember your toolbox or container. Gently place your ability:

1. to draw the earth's energy up through your feet chakras, through your legs to the base of your spine, dropping it down your grounding cord, which is as wide as your hips, your lower circuit

2. to draw your aura in around, above and below your body

3. with two roses, one on either side, and seven in front and behind parallel to each of your chakras;

4. your being sitting so comfortably in the center of your head, your unique sanctuary, your one being in your one body, in your central control

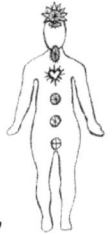

5. calling back your energy, attention and focus, filtering it along your upper circuit, replenishing each of your chakras with your life force energy

6. drawing in your warm, golden, healing energy from your higher/divine self and running it along your upper circuit breathing and flushing each of your chakras, clearing, stabilizing and healing them.

Class Seven

Cords

With a nice deep breath, gently inhale and draw the earth's energy up through your feet and drop it down your grounding cord. This is your lower circuit. Allow any irritants to drop down your grounding cord to be recycled.

Feel your feet resting on the floor. Plunk your **being** down into your chair in the center of your head. Take a look around your room. One **being** to one **body.** If you find anyone else in your room with you, say, "Hello. Go outside to the center of your own head!" Breathe. This is your unique sanctuary.

Gently allow your aura to come in around, above and below you. Place roses parallel to each of your chakras, front and back. Place a rose on either side of you at the edge of your aura. Now your body has its electromagnetic field in around it. Gently feel your higher or divine self and draw in that wonderful golden current of healing energy. Allow it to come in at the top of your head and flow down the back of your spine clearing, stabilizing and healing each of the back sides of your chakras. Allow any residue to flow out into your roses and drop down their stems to be discharged.

Allow a bit of this healing energy to flow down your grounding cord, clearing, stabilizing and healing it. As you exhale, allow this current of your healing energy to come up the front of your spine clearing, stabilizing and healing the fronts of each of your chakras. At your throat, allow this healing energy to flow across your shoulders, down your arms to your hands. Feel your hands. Allow your healing energy to come back up your arms to your throat, up across your face, washing your big picture windows flowing up and out of the top of your head and your auric field. Allow any residue to flow out to your roses and be discharged down their stems. This is your upper circuit. From the center of your head, create your filter above your head. Gently call back all of your energy, attention and focus. Allow your life force energy to return to your body and flow along your upper circuit. Your chakras will be replenished with your life force energy.

Have you considered calling back your energy, attention and focus after an event that utilized a fair bit of your energy? It could be a meeting at work, a conference with your child's teacher, an outing to your local market, a lengthy conversation, email or text with someone, a disappointing outcome, wherever we disperse our energy.

Take a moment here to just breathe. Be present in the center of your head.

~~~~~~Cords are the subject of the moment...~~~~~~

Cords are a result of the desire for communication and connection. It is how we all exchange energy every day, all the time. It does take two to tango. There is some level of agreement in the exchange of cords. This is what we are doing when we call our energy, attention and focus back. We are calling the cords we have placed into people, places and things back to ourselves!

Cords are defined as "a string of twisted strands or fibers; an insulated flexible electric wire fitted with a plug; or a long rope like structure ~ a spinal cord."

Cords will inform you about your relationships with others. You may find cords in unexpected chakras from unexpected people. We have all accumulated many cords as we have moved through life. Imagine the chakras trying to flow freely open and close, as we move through our day with all of these cords in them. Imagine a line of yarn or ribbon from one of your chakras to one of the chakras of a loved one. Then multiply these strands of ribbon by all the cords to all the chakras we each have. Truly, it is quite a tangle.

As you sit centered in your aura and the center of your head, you may choose one of these ways to view and release your cords.

You may have your body form outside of your picture window. Turn it sideways or profile to your view.

You may scoot forward on your chair. You may use your hands to feel, or gently sense, the cords in each of your chakras, front and back, as we disconnect your cords. There will be all sizes of cords.

Energy follows thought. As you hold the command in

your space, you will gently release the cords to the front and back of each chakra, move them to the edge of your aura and allow them to be returned to the donors. If a cord feels stuck, say, "Hello. Who are you from? I will be removing this connection and returning your energy to you. We may communicate on the physical if we wish." Remember, you have a lifetime accumulation of cords in each of your energy centers or chakras. Can you see, sense or feel all those ribbons or cords?

Choose your method and be gentle with yourself. Either from your view of your body or with your hands, say hello to your first chakra, at the base of your spine. If you wish, you may ask that any cords present in your first chakra be gently released, moved to the edge of your auric field and returned to the donors.

A cord in your basic survival or first chakra, may represent: someone's wish for you to help him or her survive. A child or friend who is sick or hurt. A lover who left you. The feeling "I need you" may be released. Your child who has fallen down on the school playground and immediately sends a cord for grounded reassurance.

Breathe your golden, healing energy through your first chakra as you allow these accumulated cords to be released and returned. Gently call back your energy attention and focus. Allow your life force to replenish your first chakra.

You may experience a rush of memories, pictures, tastes or smells. It is all OK. Breathe. Pat your body. Allow your hands to rest in between chakras if you are using them to feel the cords. If you are viewing, allow your hands to rest in your lap, facing up.

When you are ready, gently become aware of your second chakra. This is the energy center of sensuality, sexuality, emotion, creativity, baby-making parts. A cord here may represent "I am interested in you sexually" or "Give me your emotional support" or "Pay attention to my emotions". You may experience a needy vibration and potential energy drain on you.

If you wish, you may request that any cords present in the front and back of your second chakra gently be released, moved to the edge of your auric field and returned to the donors. Breathe. Call back your energy attention and focus. Allow your second energy center to be replenished with your life force energy.

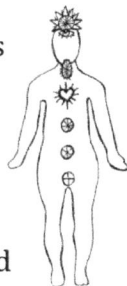

For those who are of an age where they have had sexual relations, know that any and everyone with whom you were intimate with had a cord in this chakra. With the clearing of these cords this can be a tremendous freeing up for our second chakra's flow.

When you are ready, bring your focus to your third chakra. This is the energy center of will, moving energy out into the world into form. A cord here may represent someone's wish to have some of your energy, rather than being responsible for running his or her own.

If you wish, you may request that any cords present in the front and back of your third chakra gently be released, moved to the edge of your auric field and returned to the donors. Breathe. Call back your energy attention and focus. Allow your third chakra to be replenished with your life force energy.

If you get a stomachache out of nowhere or your low back suddenly squawks at you, consider in the future, looking to see if you just were corded in your third chakra. You now have the power and ability to clear these cords and restore this area to a state of ease.

With this fourth chakra we will be halfway through disconnecting the cords. It may seem a bit overwhelming. It is a lifetime's accumulation. Once these cords are released you may experience a variety of feelings and memories. Your chakras will have the opportunity to flow freely as you move through your day. It is so worth it!

As you are ready, become aware of your fourth chakra. This is your heart center, the center of unconditional love, and affinity. We all have a collection of cords here. Our first best friend. Our first infatuation. Our first love. All of our loves. Our family. Our children.

Our friends. A cord here may represent, "I love you" or "I like you".

If you wish, you may request that any cords in the front and back of your fourth chakra gently be released, moved to the edge of your auric field and returned to the donors. Breathe. Call back your energy attention and focus. Allow your fourth chakra to be replenished with your life force energy. There may be some whom you want to have a heart cord with. When we are done, we will have the opportunity to reconnect with those whom we hold a heart connection. We will have these cords from the front of our heart to the front of their heart!

Take a nice deep cleansing breath in. Allow your body to be flushed with your upper circuit of gold. Stand up if you wish, bend over, jump up and down if you feel fidgety. Once you feel at ease again, ready yourself for your fifth chakra clearing.

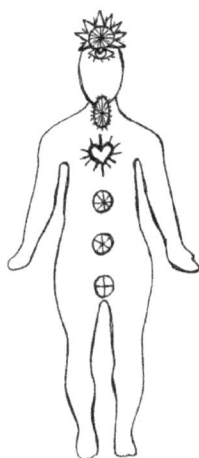

Your fifth chakra is your grand central station, your center for communication, both through your voice and through your hands. A cord here may represent, "I want to talk with you" or "Watch what you say".

If you wish, you may gently release any cords coming into the front and back of your fifth chakra, move them to the edge of your auric field and allow them to return to their donors. Breathe.

Call back your life force, energy attention and focus. Allow it to replenish your fifth chakra.

Speaking one's truth is a fifth chakra function. If you find a sudden ache in your throat or a constriction you may want to check for cords and release them.

Our sixth chakra is our energy center of clear seeing, where we experience extra sensory perceptions, our sanctuary! A cord here may represent someone else in the center of your head, "I'm thinking about you". "What are you thinking about me?" A desire to see through your eyes. A means of gathering information from and about you.

If you wish, you may gently release any cords coming into the front and back of your sixth chakra, move them to the edge of your auric field, and allow them to be returned to their donors. Call back your energy, attention and focus and allow your sixth chakra to be replenished with your life force energy.

If you find yourself with a sudden headache check your sixth chakra for any cords. Someone in the center of your head may most certainly give you a headache. This is where we say, "Hello. This is my space and I claim it. Go outside to the center of your own head!" You have seniority over your body with your being!

Ah. Our seventh chakra. This is our energy center of knowingness and intuition. A cord here may represent "I want to control you" or "I want you to follow me" or "Do it my way".

Teachers or people whom we believe know more than we may have corded with us to share information.

If you wish, you may gently disconnect any cords coming into the front and back of your seventh chakra. Release them to the edge of your auric field and allow them to be returned to their donors. Call back your energy, attention and focus and allow your seventh chakra to be replenished with your life force energy.

Own your Crown Chakra. This is your space.

There are also cords into our hand and feet chakras or energy centers.

Your hands each have their energy centers or chakras. It is where you flush your upper circuit through. Your hand energy centers facilitate your creative energy. A cord here may literally impact all that you do. A cord may represent, "Do it my way" or "Do it for me."

If you wish, you may gently release any cords coming into your hand energy centers, allowing them to move to the edge of your auric field and returning to their donors. Again gently call your energy, attention and focus back, gently flushing it down your arms and out of your hands.

Your feet energy centers are a part of your connection to the earth. A cord here may dislocate your grounding…If you wish, you may gently disconnect any cords coming into your feet energy centers, releasing them to the edge of your auric field and allowing them to be returned to their donors.

Yahoo!!!!!

Gift yourself with an enormous faucet with crystal clear water above your seventh chakra. Allow that faucet to gently flush your upper circuit. Then draw in your golden healing energy from your higher/divine self. Flush your healing energy through each of your chakras as you take slow deep breaths in and out.

Feel your aura. Have it at a comfortable distance around you. Sense, how do you feel? Breathe some more. Be aware of your lower circuit. Breathe that earth's energy up through your feet, legs and drop it down your grounding cord. Fine-tune your energy circuits and body in this time and place, your now. Reach up, stretch, bend over, touch your feet, pat your legs and sit back up in the present moment.

Know that you have just changed the game. You may hear from folks who want to know what is going on with you, what's up or just thinking about you...

Know that it is not good or bad to cord. Most folks do not understand that this is how we exchange energy all through our days. Once we become aware of this we have the opportunity to make a choice. We may disconnect cords whenever we want. We may give energy, attention and focus back to the donor and call back our own. This is healthy for both. Marylin says, "no harm or blame to you and no harm or blame to me, gently I call my energy back and give you yours."

Most of us have people that we love and wish to be connected to. You may sit in the center of your head, look out of

90

your picture window and ask those that you want to have a heart cord with, if you may. It is polite, ethical and healthy for your highest well being to ask before making your heart connection. You send your cord from the front of your heart to the front of their heart. This is how we sometimes know so clearly what another holds in their heart. We are corded with them. I want to note here that we may want to have break time from heart cords in our fourth chakra. Consider the electric plugs that are always on. There is a bit of current always being used to maintain that state of readiness. When we turn the main switch off we are allowing the circuits to curtail the flow. It is similar in our bodies. We may wish to give the heart center a rest period regularly.

This was the long version. Once we have cleared our chakras of our lifetime's worth of cords we may then go forth with the comfortable one-breath version.

This is done by sitting in the center of your head. As you draw a breath in, gently instruct that any cords coming into the front and back of all of your chakras be released, moved to the edge of your auric field and returned to the donors. As you exhale, call back your energy, attention and focus to replenish the space where the cords were removed. Your energy comes in through your filter above your head and follows your upper circuit.

Nature abhors a vacuum. If we release cords and don't fill that space in with our energy, we leave an opening for the cords to ricochet back.

Perhaps you noted that you had cords coming into the back of not only your heart, but also all of your chakras.

If we have our aura spread way out around, in front or behind us, cords more easily penetrate it. We use this ability to check out an environment or situation we are taking our body into. After gathering the information we want to bring our aura back in to a comfortable distance around our body.

One afternoon, not long after I had taken this class I was at our local market. Usually when I went I had about ten minutes to do twenty minutes worth of shopping. However on this particular afternoon, the girls were at their softball practice and I had forty-five minutes. I was making my way through the produce section. Standing in front of the red peppers I was scanning, feeling through my hand which pepper was in affinity with my need, when I became aware of a frenetic presence next to me. A hand reached over and grabbed the pepper out from underneath my hand. Hmmm. I realized that this woman was in my normal state of having to rush through the store. I took a deep breath and let go of my reaction down my grounding cord. She made a harrumph sound at me as she pushed her cart away. I scanned through the peppers and found one for us. I moved onto the bulk bins. I was bent over, getting rolled organic oats scooped into a bag, when I felt a wallop into the back of my third chakra. It made my head jerk up and turn to find the source. This wallop had penetrated right through my rose, aura and slammed into my chakra. It was the "pepper woman"! She had seen me bent over the bins and expressed an emotion as she rounded the isle with her cart. Now as I stood up, I considered what I had just experienced. This woman had no idea of the power of her thoughts. Her frustration with whatever had been directed at me. This was not all over a red pepper. I took in a deep breath. I gently gave the woman back her energy, attention and focus, her cord, and called my energy, attention and focus back to me, resetting my boundaries.

I realized several points with this encounter.

One was truly we have no idea of the power of our thoughts when backed by emotion!

Two, I would endeavor to build my consciousness about my thoughts from this point forward.

If I felt angry or frustrated I would endeavor not to direct it at a person, place or thing. I would endeavor to shift my energy. I would drop my frustration, anger or emotion down my grounding cord. Or use a giant rose out in front of me, put the emotion in the rose and blow it up! I use the word endeavor, earnest attempt, concerted effort, because it was not always my first inclination. And I use blow it up rather than the more gentle disintegrate because I have found there are times when I do want to blow up that which I have drawn out into the rose.

Your grounding cord is your physical connection to the Earth. Use it as your taproot, flusher, lightning rod or garbage chute. Remember your lower circuit, in the art of one breath.

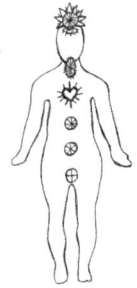

Use your , or suitcase to put a worry, fear or belief in for release.

The center of your head is your sanctuary. It is your archives and library. Your enlightenment. Past, Present and Future. No parking; this is just for you!

This art of calling back your energy, attention and focus makes more sense when we understand about cords. You now know how to disconnect cords between you and the people, places and things you have interacted with during your day. Feel your body as you call your aura in around, above and below you. Place roses in front and back of each of your chakras, hands and feet and along side you. These serve as your filters and deflectors. There are so many uses for your roses.

You have gathered in your tools, your abilities, your knowing and ability to intuit. You know how to bring your healing energy in from your higher self. Down the back of the spine and up the front, flushing each of your energy centers, putting the residue into roses, and discarding it down the stems. This is your upper circuit.

If you find yourself yawning or your eyes watering, your energy is a-flowing. You may stretch up and then bend over to dump the excess out.

Remember your CHI ball and all the creative energy that moves through your hands.

Say hello to your body.

Breathe.

Acknowledge where it is right now.

Gift yourself with something that will nurture it. A big drink of water, a walk or long soak in the tub, whatever it is that will be healthful for your body in this time and place.

Share this information that you have gathered with those you love.

Namasté

I honor the place in you

In which the entire universe dwells

I honor the place in you

Which is one of truth, love, light and peace

When you are in that place in you

And I am in that place in me

We are one.

In Bali, I have been told, this is the greeting used daily.

It is like our, "How are you doing?"

I so much enjoy Namasté

Appendix & Glossary

Definitions gathered from my handy little American Heritage Dictionary.

Amusement is defined as to cause to laugh.

Apathy is defined as lack of interest or concern in important matters.

Anger is defined as displeasure, hostility, resentment, threatening, inflamed or painful.

Aura is defined as a distinctive quality that seems to surround a person or thing, atmosphere.

Boredom is defined as to make weary by being dull, repetitive or tedious.

Chakra is defined as "wheel" from Sanskrit.

Cords are defined as a string of twisted strands or fibers; an insulated flexible wire fitted with a plug; a long ropelike structure, a spinal column.

Emotion is defined as a strong feeling; a state of mental agitation, disturbance or "jubilation, bliss", my addition.

Guilt is defined as remorseful awareness of having done something wrong, self-reproach.

Imagine is defined as to form a mental picture, conjecture, to think or fancy.

Inform is defined as to impart information to, to imbue with a quality.

Information is defined as knowledge derived from study or experience.

Joy is defined as intense or elated happiness; a source of great pleasure.

Mindful is defined as attentive, heedful, thorough, and cautious.

Resistance is defined as a force that opposes or retards motion, to strive or work against.

Tool is defined as a device, machine, means or instrument.

Validate is defined as to substantiate or verify.

Visualize is defined as to form a mental vision or image of.

Please refer to the following resources for more information:

Berkeley Psychic Institute (www.berkeleypsychic.com)
Peter Calhoun (www.petercalhoun.com)
College of San Mateo: classes with Professor Esteva
Chayo Wilson (www.chayo.biz)
Barbara Rainforth (rainforthstudio.com)
Mark Takata (marktakata.com)
Marilyn Watteyne of Jemez Springs, NM, USA
Dr. Sarah Slaughter (www.drslaughter.com)
Michaele Benedict of Montara, CA, USA
Darryl Brock of Phoenix, AZ, USA

In remembrance of:
Lewis S. Bostwick (1918-1995)
Karen Wasco (1947-1995)

www.ingramcontent.com/pod-product-compliance
Lightning Source LLC
Chambersburg PA
CBHW022306060426
42446CB00007BA/727